D1613655

PERSONAL FREEDOM & CIVIC DUTY ™

UNDERSTANDING
EQUAL RIGHTS

CORONA BREZINA

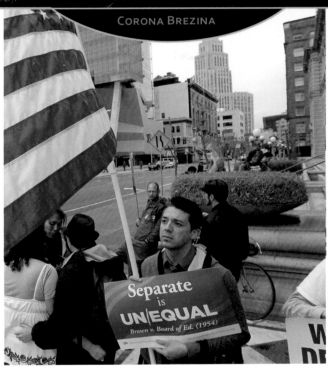

Separate
is
UN|EQUAL
Brown v. Board of Ed. (1954)

ROSEN
PUBLISHING®

New York

Published in 2014 by The Rosen Publishing Group, Inc.
29 East 21st Street, New York, NY 10010

Library of Congress Cataloging-in-Publication Data

Brezina, Corona.
Understanding equal rights/Corona Brezina.
    p. cm.—(Personal freedom and civic duty)
Includes bibliographical references and index.
ISBN 978-1-4488-9463-5 (library binding)
1. Equality before the law—United States.
2. Civil rights—United States. I. Title.
KF4764.B74 2013
342.7308'5—dc23

                                                2012040034

Manufactured in the United States of America

CPSIA Compliance Information: Batch #S13YA: For further information, contact Rosen Publishing, New York, New York, at 1-800-237-9932.

CONTENTS

INTRODUCTION

Equality is a cherished principle for citizens of the United States. The American commitment to equality dates back to the 1776 Declaration of Independence, which declares "that all men are created equal." That statement offered a stark contrast to the social system in Great Britain, where an aristocracy lived a privileged existence far removed from the circumstances of ordinary Britons.

The American Constitution laid the groundwork for equal rights in the United States, including the possible future expansion of rights. The powerful Bill of Rights established

At a Washington, D.C., rally in 2012, protesters call for the arrest of the neighborhood watch volunteer George Zimmerman, who shot and killed unarmed teenager Trayvon Martin in Florida.

many of these liberties and guaranteed Americans protection from government tyranny. Nonetheless, African Americans were excluded from basic rights until after the Civil War (1861–1865). Women were only gradually granted equal rights and finally achieved the right to vote in 1920. Discrimination, however, prevented any minority group from fully exercising equal rights.

This situation changed during the civil rights era of the mid-twentieth century. Within a span of two decades, landmark legislation and court cases vastly expanded equal rights. The era brought legal prohibitions against discrimination and opened up new opportunities for African Americans, women, Hispanics, people who were disabled, and gays. Activists such as Martin Luther King Jr., Cesar Chavez, and Gloria Steinem led these rights movements.

The civil rights era saw many victories, but equal rights battles continue today. Women still receive lower pay than men. Gays are still denied the right to marry. Some racial minorities are more likely to live in poverty.

Occasionally, high-profile instances of injustice focus public awareness on the issue of inequality. A particularly tragic event of 2012 brought renewed attention to the issue of racial discrimination. Trayvon Martin, an African American teenager in Florida, was shot and killed by George Zimmerman, a local neighborhood watch member. Police did not charge Zimmerman for the shooting until a national outcry demanded action. Investigation into Florida's "stand your ground" law found that people who claimed self-defense in killing an African American were significantly more likely to get off without legal penalties than those who killed a white person. Public opinion was also split. A poll showed that African Americans were twice as likely as whites to believe that race was a factor in the shooting. The incident revealed that despite all the progress that has advanced equal rights, Americans continue to be divided by race.

Nevertheless, equal rights benefit all Americans, not just minorities. Equal rights accord every citizen the opportunity to live to his or her full potential. The expansion of equal rights throughout American history is a success story that will continue to unfold during the twenty-first century.

WHAT ARE EQUAL RIGHTS?

CHAPTER 1

The concept of equal rights—the right of all people to be treated equally—is one of the cornerstones of democracy. A person cannot legally be denied access to the rights granted to the majority of Americans on the basis of race, religion, sex, age, disability status, or national origin. Many people take their rights for granted, but equal rights today represent the victories of hard battles fought by activists in past eras.

Equal rights are continually expanding and changing. Most people living in the early twentieth century would find it unbelievable that one hundred years later, women, racial minorities, people who are disabled, and other minority groups would all be considered equals in the view of the law and American society.

Laws and court rulings reflect this progress. In the 1989 case of *Stanford v. Kentucky*, for example, the U.S. Supreme Court upheld the death sentence for an offender who had been seventeen years old when he committed a murder. In *Roper v. Simmons* (2005), however, the Court ruled against imposing the death sentence

An equal rights amendment to the Constitution was first proposed in 1923, but it was never passed by Congress. Nearly a century later, some activists still support the proposed amendment.

on another offender who had been seventeen years old when he committed a murder. One of the grounds for the ruling was that the death sentence for juveniles constituted cruel and unusual punishment, an argument that had been rejected in *Stanford*. The verdict also referred to "the necessity of referring to 'the evolving standards of decency that mark the progress of a maturing society' to determine which punishments are so disproportionate as to be 'cruel and unusual.'" In other words, times had changed.

"Equal rights" is an imprecise term that can have different meanings in different contexts. For many women, the equal rights movement was the women's rights campaign for a constitutional amendment granting equal rights to women. Sometimes "equal rights" refers to the civil rights of a nation; sometimes it refers to legal equality under the law. Used in a broader sense, "equal rights" may describe the human rights accorded to all human beings.

CIVIL RIGHTS

Civil rights are the personal liberties granted to citizens of a nation regardless of their race, color, religion, sex, age, disability, or national origin. When people are treated differently because of any of these criteria, it is an example of discrimination and a violation of civil rights. Laws such as the Civil Rights Act of 1964 describe the specific civil rights protections accorded to all Americans.

One of the most basic civil rights in society is the right to vote. When the United States was founded, only white male property owners—fewer than one out of five Americans—possessed the right to vote.

Americans' civil rights also prohibit discrimination in education, employment, and housing. All students must be given equal access to education. Schools cannot be segregated by race, and disabled students must be provided with educational support that meets their needs. In the workplace, employers are prohibited from discriminating in matters concerning hiring, pay, promotion, and treatment on the job. People selling or renting out housing cannot discriminate against buyers or renters.

Every American is guaranteed certain civil rights regarding the criminal justice system, many of them derived from the Bill of Rights. Some restrict police authority, such as the limits on search and seizure. Others grant protections in the courtroom, such as the right against self-incrimination and the right to an attorney. One of the most famous legal rights is the right to remain silent, known as the Miranda warning. It is named for the landmark 1966 U.S. Supreme Court case of *Miranda v. Arizona,* in which the Court ruled that police must inform a suspect of his or her rights before interrogation.

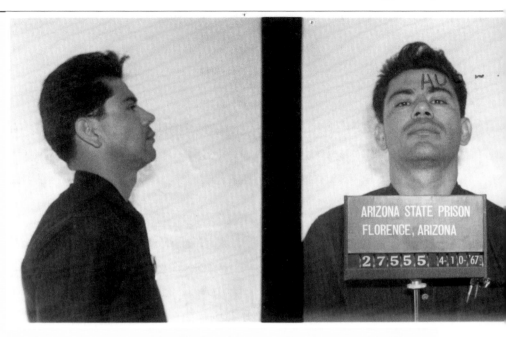

Ernest Miranda confessed to a 1963 crime during interrogation. The U.S. Supreme Court overturned his subsequent conviction because the police had not informed him of his constitutional rights.

Many people immediately associate the term "civil rights" with the African American civil rights movement that brought about an avalanche of reform. Other minority groups also launched rights movements during that period, many of them inspired by the civil rights victories occurring across the country.

EQUALITY BEFORE THE LAW

The concept of legal equality requires that the justice system apply the law equally to all people. This is

THE EQUAL RIGHTS AMENDMENT

Many people strongly associate the phrase "equal rights" with the unsuccessful fight by the women's rights movement to pass an Equal Rights Amendment (ERA) to the Constitution. The proposed text states, "Equality of rights under the law shall not be denied or abridged by the United States or by any state on account of sex."

Supporters of the ERA point out that the Constitution does not specifically grant women equality with men under the law. The Nineteenth Amendment grants women the right to vote, but it does not address any other legal rights of women. The Supreme Court has cited the Equal Protection Clause of the Fourteenth Amendment in striking down cases of legal discrimination against women, but this amendment does not provide the clear and explicit equal protection as the proposed ERA. Today, discrimination against women is covered by a patchwork of different laws that vary from state to state. The ERA would facilitate decisions on sex discrimination cases and provide women with legal security in matters such as family law, education, workplace opportunities, Social Security coverage, and much more.

derived from the due process guarantee in the Fifth Amendment.

In addition, according to the equal protection clause of the Fourteenth Amendment, the law itself cannot discriminate in its application. In the milestone 1967 case of *Loving v. Virginia*, the Supreme

Court struck down a law banning interracial marriages. By denying the freedom to marry on racially discriminatory grounds, the Virginia law violated the principle of equality in the Fourteenth Amendment.

The Fourteenth Amendment only gradually extended equal protection to women, but the Equal Protection Clause has been cited in cases involving different treatment between sexes in the law. The case *Craig v. Boren* (1976), for example, struck down a state law that set the minimum drinking age at twenty-one for men and eighteen for women.

HUMAN RIGHTS

Equal rights can also refer to human rights—the rights inherent to all human beings. Unlike civil rights and legal rights, which vary according to a country's laws, human rights are considered to be universal. Everyone in the world is entitled to certain human rights.

The most definitive statement of human rights is the 1948 Universal Declaration of Human Rights adopted by the United Nations (UN) General Assembly. The UN was founded in 1945, the same year that World War II ended. In 1948, many of the member nations were still struggling to recover from the effects of the war. In the drafting of the declaration, the memories of the horrors of war and its

First Lady Eleanor Roosevelt served as the first chairperson of the U.S. Commission on Human Rights. She was highly influential in drafting the Universal Declaration of Human Rights.

consequences on ordinary people were still fresh in everyone's minds.

The Universal Declaration addresses a wide range of rights. The first article begins with the statement that "All human beings are born free and equal in dignity and rights." The opening articles cover the rights of the individual, and the later ones move on to describe broad rights concerning culture, community, and social order. Some of the basic rights in the Universal Declaration include life and liberty, food and housing, property, equality, legal rights, education, marriage, privacy, freedom of movement, paid employment, religious freedom, free speech, freedom of assembly, participation in government, and freedom from enslavement, torture, and discrimination.

In the decades since its passage, the Universal Declaration has been hugely influential. Oppressed people have cited its terms in appealing for recognition of their rights. It has been incorporated in national constitutions and served for a model for subsequent human rights treaties. Every UN member nation, including the United States, has ratified the document, meaning that they endorse its ideals.

HISTORY OF EQUAL RIGHTS

The world has seen marvelous advances in technology and science since the founding of the United States. Equally crucial are the expanded rights granted to all Americans. In the past, discriminatory laws and practices limited the opportunities and dreams of many Americans. An examination of the history of equal rights reveals the freedoms that Americans enjoy today are truly extraordinary.

The first victory for the rights of ordinary people in Western society took place in Great Britain long before the founding of the United States. The Magna Carta, enacted in 1215, established the basis of some legal rights that were eventually incorporated into the American Constitution. In 1628, the Petition of Right increased the rights granted to the English, and the list was further expanded with the 1689 English bill of rights. By the time the United States declared independence from Britain in 1776, precedents for individual liberties had already been established.

THE DECLARATION OF INDEPENDENCE AND EQUAL RIGHTS

Thomas Jefferson drafted the Declaration of Independence. He did not set out to break new ground in personal liberties, but the opening of the second paragraph is one of the most recognizable statements in any American historical document:

> We hold these truths to be self-evident, that all men are created equal, that they are endowed by their Creator with certain unalienable Rights, that among these are Life, Liberty and the pursuit of Happiness.

More than two hundred years later, Jefferson's rights still hold the ring of truth for Americans.

Jefferson also demonstrated foresight in his original draft of the Declaration of Independence. He had included a statement condemning slavery. Some of his colleagues, however, convinced him to delete the section to avoid provoking slaveholders and tradesmen. In addition, Jefferson remained an advocate for personal liberties his entire life (despite owning more than six hundred slaves throughout his lifetime). He supported the inclusion of the Bill of Rights in the Constitution, and he developed principles of religious freedom and toleration.

A preliminary draft of the 1776 Declaration of Independence in Thomas Jefferson's handwriting includes minor revisions written in by fellow Founding Fathers John Adams and Benjamin Franklin.

Nevertheless, the concept of rights in the Declaration of Independence is narrow compared to the equal rights granted to modern Americans. Women, slaves, and Native Americans were excluded from basic rights such as voting, as were men who did not own property. Broad access to the full rights for all hinted at in the Declaration of Independence did not occur until the twentieth century.

THE CONSTITUTION AND EQUAL RIGHTS

In the early years of independence, the United States was governed by a document called the Articles of Confederation. It became obvious that a stronger central government was required if the nation were to survive. In 1787, the leading statesmen of the day gathered in Philadelphia, Pennsylvania, to draft a new document. Despite intense debate, they succeeded in agreeing on the provisions in the Constitution and signed the final version. The next step was the ratification, or approval, of the Constitution by individual states.

Some states, however, were wary of approving the new document unless it included a bill of rights. It would protect citizens' liberties and guarantee that the nation's government would never become tyrannical.

A few states made the addition of a bill of rights a condition for ratification.

James Madison undertook the task of drafting the Bill of Rights. Madison was more interested in facilitating ratification of the Constitution than in expanding equal rights. He consulted historical documents for precedents and consulted with other leaders. In total, he drew up twelve proposed amendments, two of which were eventually rejected. The Constitution was approved by Congress and ratified by enough states to go into effect in 1791. The United States was the first nation to establish a framework of government in an original constitution.

Like the Declaration of Independence, the Constitution failed to expand the rights of women or slaves. A few of the provisions in the Constitution were blatantly discriminatory against slaves. Nor did the Constitution grant Native Americans any legal rights or property rights.

The Bill of Rights serves to protect the rights of U.S. citizens from actions taken by the federal government. Most of the amendments remain relevant in the twenty-first century, and many continue to be debated and reinterpreted in court cases today. They also continue to provoke controversy. The First Amendment (which protects free speech, among other liberties) has sparked contentious debate. The Supreme Court hears cases involving First Amendment rights almost yearly. New questions on its application have arisen in the information age of Internet publishing and social media.

Other amendments protect against unreasonable search and seizure, double jeopardy (being tried twice for the same crime), self-incrimination, and cruel and unusual punishment. They also guarantee due process of the law, property ownership, and various rights involving court proceedings. Significantly, the Ninth Amendment acknowledges that there might be additional rights that should be respected by the Constitution beyond those included in the Bill of Rights.

EQUAL RIGHTS IN THE NINETEENTH CENTURY

Equal rights were not expanded in the Constitution until the adoption of the Thirteenth Amendment in 1865, the year the Civil War ended. The amendment abolished slavery and involuntary servitude and granted Congress the power of enforcement. In 1866, Congress passed the Civil Rights Act, which granted equal protection concerning property ownership, lawsuits, contracts, and several related rights. It did not, however, include penalties for violations.

In 1868, the Fourteenth Amendment reaffirmed the rights of African Americans. Among its provisions is that "nor shall any state deprive any person of life,

A student talks about the significance of the Thirteenth Amendment, which is shown here in a handwritten copy signed by Abraham Lincoln. The amendment bans slavery or involuntary servitude for Americans of all races.

liberty, or property, without due process of law; nor deny to any person within its jurisdiction the equal protection of the laws." The Fifteenth Amendment, ratified in 1870, prohibited limiting the right to vote on the basis of race. Despite these advances, the law was not strictly enforced, and African Americans frequently experienced discrimination and voting restrictions.

The U.S. Supreme Court

All three branches of the U.S. government—executive (the president), legislative (Congress), and judicial (the courts)—bear responsibility for ensuring that no Americans are deprived of equal rights. The legislative branch enacts legislation. The executive branch implements and enforces legislation passed by Congress. In addition, the president can issue executive orders, although these must comply with the law.

The courts interpret laws, determine if they are constitutional, and apply their findings to decisions in court cases. The U.S. Supreme Court is the nation's highest court. Supreme Court justices are nominated by the president and confirmed by Congress. They are appointed for life and, therefore, do not have to campaign for reelection or worry about the popularity of their rulings. No other U.S. court can overturn Supreme Court rulings, although the Court itself occasionally reverses past rulings. Many milestones in the fight for equal rights were the result of Supreme Court decisions.

Although Congress cannot override a Supreme Court decision, it can effectively nullify verdicts through legislation. In the 2007 case of *Ledbetter* v. *Goodyear Tire & Rubber Co.*, for example, the Court rejected an employee lawsuit citing the Civil Rights Act of 1964 on the grounds that the act imposed a 180-day filing deadline. In reaction, Congress passed the Lilly Ledbetter Fair Pay Act of 2009 that amended the Civil Rights Act and President Barack Obama signed it into law.

In addition, the courts took little action to defend or advance equal rights throughout the nineteenth century. In the infamous 1857 case of *Dred Scott v. Sanford*, the Court's ruling restricted the rights of African Americans. As state legislatures passed laws that limited the rights of African Americans, lower courts in some states issued rulings that rejected the principles of the Civil Rights Act of 1866. In *United States v. Cruikshank* (1876), the Supreme Court ruled that although racial discrimination by government officials was prohibited, discrimination by individuals was lawful. In 1875, Congress passed the Second Civil Rights Act, which safeguarded all Americans regardless of race in access to public accommodations and facilities and protected the right to serve on juries, but it was declared unconstitutional by the Supreme Court in 1883.

EQUAL RIGHTS IN THE TWENTIETH CENTURY

Unlike the Supreme Court of the nineteenth century, the Court during the following century greatly expanded the personal freedoms of American citizens. The first major rights victory of the twentieth century occurred in 1920 with the ratification of the Nineteenth Amendment, which granted women the right to vote. Two other amendments ratified during

The ratification of the Nineteenth Amendment in 1920 granted women the right to vote and represented victory for the women's suffrage movement, which had begun in the mid-nineteenth century.

the twentieth century also addressed the right to vote. The Twenty-fourth Amendment (1964) prohibited poll taxes, which some states enacted in an attempt to suppress voting. The Twenty-sixth Amendment (1970) lowered the voting age from twenty-one to eighteen years old.

During the mid-twentieth century, equal rights were broadened during the era known as the civil rights movement. It is sometimes called the African American civil rights movement because glaring injustices to African Americans initially propelled the movement, but many other minority groups also gained substantial rights. The Supreme Court ruling in the case of *Brown v. Board of Education of Topeka* (1954), which struck down school segregation, is considered by many to be the event that sparked the movement. The landmark legislation and court rulings of the 1960s and 1970s established many of the rights that Americans today cherish or, regrettably, take for granted.

The 1980s, with new leaders and a new atmosphere in government, saw a slowdown in the pace of the expansion of rights. Nevertheless, the courts have continued to uphold the liberties gained during the civil rights era.

RIGHTS OF AFRICAN AMERICANS

W hen the United States declared independence from Great Britain in 1776, the nation had a population of 2.5 million people, 575,000 of whom were African Americans. All but forty thousand of these were slaves, most of them held by plantation owners in the South.

At that time, Americans were already deeply conflicted over the issue of slavery. Some people held that the statement in the Declaration of Independence "that all men are created equal" included African Americans. Racism was widespread among white Americans, however, and even many opponents of slavery did not favor the idea of granting equal rights to African Americans.

Following the American Revolution, the northern states moved to abolish slavery. Southern states remained firm in their commitment to slavery and tightened oppression of free African Americans. They were treated differently under the law from whites, and racial segregation grew common.

CHAPTER 3

THE STRUGGLE OVER SLAVERY

The U.S. Constitution reflects the conflict over the issue of slavery. Southerners at the Constitutional Convention steadfastly supported the institution, and northerners were willing to compromise to reach an agreement. Although the word "slavery" never appears in the document, three clauses restrict the rights of slaves. Article I, Section 2, states that slaves could be counted as three-fifths of a person in tallying population for purposes such as taxation. Article I, Section 9, stated that the slave trade could not be abolished before 1808. Article IV, Section 2, required that escaped slaves who crossed into another state be returned to their owners.

Friction over the issue of slavery continued to build into the nineteenth century. In the North, abolitionists harshly condemned the institution of slavery. Nonetheless, free African Americans in northern states lacked equal rights, such as the right to vote. Discrimination was commonly accepted, and African Americans were often segregated from whites in schools, businesses, and other institutions. In the South, the practice of slavery grew more entrenched. The slave population increased to nearly two million by the time of the outbreak of the Civil War, and the southern economy became highly dependent on slave labor.

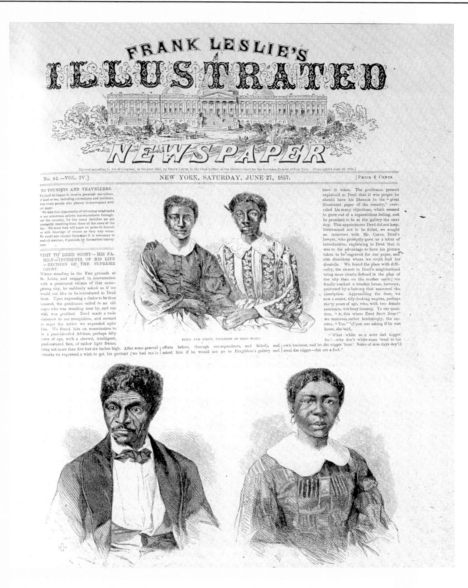

A newspaper from 1857 covers the impact of the *Dred Scott* decision, in which the Supreme Court ruled that a slave could not attain freedom by entering a non-slave state.

As the rift over slavery between the North and the South grew deeper, many southern states passed harsh laws supporting slavery and discriminating against free African Americans. The Fugitive Slave Act of 1850, which required that northerners help recover slaves who escaped from the South, helped deepen northern opposition to slavery.

In 1857, the Supreme Court issued a ruling in the case of *Dred Scott v. Sandford* that ignited a furor of debate and opposition. Dred Scott was a slave battling for his freedom. The Court ruled that African Americans could not be considered U.S. citizens and that they were not granted any rights under the Constitution. The *Dred Scott* decision also stated that Congress had no authority to ban slavery in states or territories.

Abraham Lincoln was elected president in 1860 without winning an electoral vote from any southern states. After the Civil War broke out in 1861, public opinion in the North turned strongly against slavery. In 1863, Lincoln issued the Emancipation Proclamation, which freed all slaves in Confederate territory.

THE END OF SLAVERY

After the Civil War ended in 1865 with a Union victory, slavery was legally abolished. The Thirteenth Amendment to the Constitution outlawed slavery, and

Demonstrators march in 1979 to mark the twenty-fifth anniversary of the landmark *Brown* ruling that banned school segregation by race. Today, racial disparities in public education remain a controversial issue.

the Fourteenth Amendment gave African Americans citizenship and legal rights. The Fifteenth Amendment granted citizens the right to vote and stated that the right could not be denied because of "race, color or previous condition of servitude."

Despite this victory for African Americans, they were still far from achieving full equality, especially in the South. Congress passed several civil rights acts in the decade following the Civil War. Support for the rights of African Americans dwindled as public interest moved on to new issues, however. Congress did not pass further civil rights legislation until the 1950s. During this period, political leaders in the South paid little regard to the new constitutional rights granted to African Americans. Segregation became ingrained and discriminatory laws took away the right to vote for many African Americans. Hate groups such as the Ku Klux Klan emerged to intimidate African Americans who protested the injustice of their situation. The

THE CIVIL RIGHTS ACT OF 1964

On July 2, 1964, President Lyndon B. Johnson signed the Civil Rights Act into law. It outlawed discrimination on the basis of race, color, religion, gender, or national origin. It ended segregation in businesses and public places and prohibited discrimination in voter registration and employment. It also laid the foundations for more civil rights legislation.

Congress took up the Civil Rights Act in response to a call to action from President John F. Kennedy. Following protests and racial violence during the summer of 1963, Kennedy gave a speech urging the enactment of anti-discriminatory measures. He and congressional leaders drafted the act, but Kennedy was assassinated in November before the bill came up for a vote.

Powerful factions in both the House of Representatives and the Senate opposed the act. A committee in the House tried to keep the bill from coming up for a vote. Opponents in the Senate blocked the legislation with a filibuster. They finally agreed to support a compromise version of the bill, which was approved by a wide margin in the House and the Senate.

1896 Supreme Court case of *Plessy v. Ferguson* ruled that racial segregation did not violate the Constitution. After this decision, segregation became much more widespread in the South.

In 1909, the National Association for the Advancement of Colored People (NAACP) was organized to fight for equal rights. The group took legal action against racist policies and it organized protests. Despite many significant victories for racial equality, the Supreme Court fell short of overruling the *Plessy v. Ferguson* decision.

THE CIVIL RIGHTS MOVEMENT

The fight for equal rights gained national prominence in the mid-1950s. In 1954, the Supreme Court decided in the landmark case of *Brown v. Board of Education of Topeka* that school segregation violated the Fourteenth Amendment. The case marked the end of state-supported segregation, known as Jim Crow laws. Further Supreme Court rulings reversed the *Plessy v. Ferguson* decision.

In 1955, black seamstress Rosa Parks refused to give up her seat to a white man on a bus in Montgomery, Alabama. Her arrest sparked a boycott of Montgomery's segregated public transit system that was organized by Martin Luther King Jr., who gained recognition as a national leader of the civil rights movement during the campaign. King's philosophy of

In his 1963 "I Have a Dream" speech, Martin Luther King Jr. hoped that someday his children would "not be judged by the color of their skin but by the content of their character."

nonviolent resistance and his success in mobilizing for racial equality inspired many other groups to organize marches, protests, sit-ins, and other forms of demonstration. In 1963, more than two hundred thousand people flocked to Washington, D.C., for the March on Washington for Jobs and Freedom, which culminated with King's "I Have a Dream" speech.

Lawmakers responded to the pressure. The Civil Rights Act of 1957 supported African Americans' right to vote, and its provisions were expanded by a subsequent act in 1960. The landmark Civil Rights Act of 1964 prohibited the segregation of and discrimination against African Americans and other minority groups. The Voting Rights Act of 1965 introduced measures to ensure that minority groups would be able to exercise their right to vote. The Civil Rights Act of 1968 included the Fair Housing Act, which prohibited discrimination in selling and renting homes.

The African American civil rights movement faltered after the assassination of King in 1968. The reasons for the slowing of momentum went beyond the loss of a leader. The movement lost focus after achieving so many of its goals. Many whites withdrew from the movement, either because of the violence that had occurred in many cities or because they moved onto new causes, such as environmental activism or women's rights. The political atmosphere had changed as well. President Richard Nixon, elected in 1968, was less supportive of civil rights measures than his predecessors.

One significant measure included in the civil rights acts of the 1960s was the introduction of affirmative action. Affirmative action went beyond prohibiting discrimination against minorities; it encouraged taking steps to increase minority representation in businesses, schools, and other institutions. The rationale was that affirmative action would compensate for

In February 2012, students in California support overturning Proposition 209, a ban on affirmative action in state institutions that was passed by California voters in 1996. The Ninth U.S. Circuit Court of Appeals, in April 2012, ruled against repealing the measure, in which it is forbidden to consider race in admissions decisions at public universities.

historical disadvantages experienced by minorities and correct underrepresentation of minorities in schools and the workplace.

Affirmative action has proven to be controversial, especially in education. Opponents hold that it is a form of reverse discrimination against whites. The courts have responded by limiting the scope of affirmative action. In *Regents of the University of*

California v. Bakke (1978), the Supreme Court struck down the practice of reserving places for minority students in colleges.

Advocates of affirmative action maintain that in addition to helping members of minority groups, the policy has the positive effect of promoting diversity in institutions and society. In 2003, the Court upheld the use of race as a factor in school admissions in the case of *Grutter v. Bollinger*. In 2011, guidelines issued by the administration of President Barack Obama encouraged colleges and universities to promote racial diversity.

RIGHTS OF OTHER
RACIAL MINORITIES

The African American civil rights movement of the mid-twentieth century was the most epic and turbulent fight for racial equality, but other racial minority groups have also faced discrimination in the United States and worked to overcome it.

The statutes of the civil rights era swept away the major legal barriers standing in the way of racial equality. These laws also granted equality under the law to women and other minority groups.

ASIAN AMERICANS

Many Asian Americans identify more strongly with their country of origin than the broad categorization of "Asian American" implies. For example, they view themselves as Chinese American or Korean American. Most arrived during distinct waves of immigration occurring at various periods throughout American history. Each group has faced unique challenges depending on current laws and public sentiment at the time of their arrival.

In 1942, as World War II was being fought overseas, many Japanese Americans were confined in internment camps. Here, a little girl awaits a bus that will convey her family to a camp.

Chinese immigrants were the first Asian group to arrive in large numbers. In the mid-nineteenth century, after gold was discovered in California, Chinese workers were encouraged to immigrate and fill much-needed jobs in the United States. Chinese laborers notably completed much of the construction of the transcontinental railroad in the West. They faced hostility and discrimination, however, and they saw their rights gradually restricted. Discriminatory laws forced them from their jobs, and schools became segregated.

Emigration from China was cut off, separating many immigrants from their wives and families. Restrictions were not loosened until 1943.

The first Japanese to immigrate to the United States were recruited to work on agricultural plantations in Hawaii during the late nineteenth century. After Hawaii became a U.S. territory, many moved to the West Coast. As with the Chinese, Japanese immigrants became the target of animosity and saw their rights restricted. The harshest treatment of Japanese Americans, however, occurred during World War II (1939–1945). Since Japan was the declared enemy of the United States, the U.S. government questioned the loyalty of Japanese Americans. About 120,000 Japanese, many of them U.S. citizens and nearly half of whom were children, were held in internment camps. In 1948, and again in 1988, the government issued reimbursement and compensation to Japanese Americans who had been interned.

Changes in immigration laws in 1965 opened the United States to further Asian immigration. Newer immigrants did not have to face the ingrained discrimination experienced by earlier arrivals. Immigrants came from India, Korea, and the Philippines. After the Vietnam War ended in 1975, a wave of refugees arrived from Vietnam and Southeast Asia.

Overall, Asian Americans are well educated, earn high incomes, and do not report high rates of discrimination, according to a 2012 Pew Research Center report. Recent immigrants from Southeast Asia, however, are more likely to be undereducated and have to live in poverty.

HISPANIC AMERICANS

Hispanic Americans are united by their common language of Spanish. They comprise a diverse group of different nationalities, cultures, and races. Today, many Hispanics say that they experience discrimination because of the prejudice against illegal immigrants.

Hispanics have a centuries-long history in the United States. Spaniards governed Florida, Texas, and several southwestern states long before the British established the American colonies. When the areas became U.S. territories, tens of thousands of Hispanics living there became American nationals.

As with Asian Americans, different groups of Hispanic immigrants have arrived in distinct waves. About one hundred thousand Cubans came to the United States during the nineteenth century, and another influx streamed in after Fidel Castro took power in Cuba in 1959. Puerto Rico is a U.S. territory, and Puerto Ricans were granted U.S. citizenship in

The 2012 DREAM Act allows young undocumented immigrants to avoid deportation and legally obtain work. Here, young people fill out their applications at an immigrant rights center.

1917, which allows Puerto Ricans to migrate easily to the United States. Most of the Hispanic population arrived in a huge wave since the 1970s, as immigrants from Mexico and Central America swarmed to the United States.

Mexican Americans make up the largest group of Hispanics in the United States. Hundreds of thousands of Mexicans immigrated to the United States during the late nineteenth and early twentieth century, but many returned to Mexico during the Great Depression of the 1930s.

Like other minority groups, Mexican Americans were subjected to discrimination and segregation. The 1945 case *Méndez v. Westminster School District*, in which a U.S. Court of Appeals ruled against school segregation for Mexican American children, preceded the groundbreaking *Brown v. Board of Education* case. During the fight for civil rights in the 1960s, activist Cesar Chavez became the most important civil rights leader in the Southwest. A former farmworker, Chavez established a farmworkers' union and used strikes and other nonviolent means of protest to improve working conditions for agricultural laborers.

The spike in immigration during the later twentieth century—especially illegal immigration—prompted proposals of measures that targeted illegal immigrants and restricted immigration. In 1994, a drastic ballot measure in California's election brought the issue to national prominence. Proposition 187 called for a ban on illegal immigrants receiving public social services, including health care and education. Voters approved the measure by a wide margin. Implementation was blocked in court, however, and California's governor did not appeal the decision.

Immigration reform became a major political issue during the first decade of the twenty-first century. Congress debated immigration reform measures during 2006 and 2007, but the House and Senate were unable to reach agreement. The main point of contention was how to deal with the millions of illegal immigrants residing in the nation. Any plan that provided a path to citizenship proved unpopular on the grounds that it rewarded the violation of immigration laws.

In 2012, President Barack Obama's administration introduced a program shielding young immigrants

ARIZONA V. UNITED STATES (2012)

In 2010, Arizona enacted the nation's harshest law targeting illegal immigrants. It required that police check immigration status when detaining a person for a traffic stop or any other reason. It also made it a crime for an immigrant to be in Arizona without carrying documentation, made it a crime for illegal immigrants to seek work, and gave police more power to arrest suspected illegal immigrants. Several other states quickly followed Arizona's lead in enacting measures intended to restrict illegal immigration.

The law immediately sparked an outcry, nation-wide protests, and boycotts of Arizona. The U.S. Department of Justice quickly challenged the legality of the law. The Supreme Court eventually heard the case in 2011. In 2012, the Court ruling struck down three parts of the law on the grounds that they interfered with congressional authority. The Court allowed the provision on checking immigration status of people stopped for another violation to stand.

who arrived in the United States illegally as children from deportation. Under the Deferred Action for Childhood Arrivals initiative, eligible immigrants would be granted temporary, renewable work permits.

NATIVE AMERICANS

Native Americans occupy a unique position among racial minority groups in the United States. They have fought for civil rights as American citizens, but they have also fought for treaty rights as members of sovereign American Indian nations.

After Europeans began settling the present-day United States, conflicts quickly arose with the native peoples. As settlers moved westward into Native American land, they easily conquered their foes with superior weaponry. By the second half of the nineteenth century, most Native Americans had been conquered and were resettled on reservations. The subjugation and forced migration of Native Americans was brutal and tragic.

Many laws passed during the late nineteenth century, such as the Indian Appropriations Act of 1871, further stripped away the rights of Native Americans to govern their own affairs. The General Allotment Act of 1887 enabled the federal government to sell off reservation land without full consent of the tribe. When the practice was challenged in the 1903 case *Lone Wolf v. Hitchcock*, the Supreme Court upheld the government position rather than recognize the property rights of Native Americans. The U.S. government also promoted the assimilation of Native Americans, which in many cases led to children being taken away from their families and raised in boarding schools. Native Americans who weren't already citizens gained citizenship with the American Citizenship Act of 1924, but they continued to hold allegiance to their tribal leadership.

In 1928, a government report detailed the poor standards of living of most Native Americans. Measures in the Indian Reorganization Act (IRA) of 1934 enacted reform policies that restored some autonomy to tribal governments. A fresh attack on treaty rights began again during the 1950s, however. A new policy called "termination" aimed to bring an end to Native American dependence on government services. The government seized land and many Native Americans were relocated to cities, which often proved a traumatizing experience. The policy ceased in 1960, but it had the effect of raising awareness among Native Americans of civil rights issues.

The civil rights acts and voting rights acts of the 1960s included protections specifically for Native Americans. The 1968 Civil Rights Act, in particular, included an Indian Civil Rights Act that extended many of the liberties in the Bill of Rights to Native

Members of a coalition of Southwestern Indian tribes sing an AIM song outside a California courthouse in 2006. The group sued over a proposed ski resort expansion onto sacred land.

Americans. This legislation proved controversial because it restricted tribal sovereignty. A 1978 case, *Santa Clara Pueblo v. Martinez*, reduced the authority of the Indian Civil Rights Act by rejecting government enforcement of laws over tribal governments.

Since the 1960s, Native Americans have continued to fight for their treaty rights and preserve their culture and religion. A militant rights group called the American Indian Movement (AIM) brought attention to the plight of Native Americans during the 1970s. In 1975, partially as a result of AIM's activism, the government granted Native Americans greater power in governing their own affairs with the Indian Self-Determination and Education Assistance Act.

One of the most pressing and persistent issues for Native Americans is addressing the deep poverty that spawns crime, violence against women, substance abuse, poor health, and lost educational opportunities on reservations. Since the 1970s, some Native American tribes have opened casinos, which have brought in much-needed revenue.

WOMEN'S RIGHTS

CHAPTER 5

I n 1840, abolitionists from Great Britain and the United States gathered in London for the World Anti-Slavery Convention. Some of the most ardent American activists in the movement were women. But the organizers refused to allow women to speak or even sit in the main audience. Women were seated together off to the side of the main hall behind a curtain.

Today, it may seem outrageous that the experienced women activists were sidelined, but women back then were accustomed to their subordinate position. In nineteenth-century America, a woman's role was primarily that of wife and mother. Women were not allowed to vote, and married women could not own property or sign contracts. Very few women worked outside the home—especially married women—and job options were limited.

Not surprisingly, some of the women at the convention discussed their treatment at the convention and, more generally, women's position in society. Two of the women, Lucretia Mott and Elizabeth Cady Stanton, agreed that they should organize a convention about women's rights.

THE RIGHT TO VOTE

The Seneca Falls Convention opened on July 19, 1848. About three hundred people, including forty men, arrived on the first day. They discussed issues such as property and divorce laws, access to jobs and education, and the controversial question of suffrage— the right to vote. The organizers had drafted a Declaration of Sentiments based on the Declaration of Independence. Part of the Declaration was a list of twelve resolutions on women's issues, including one that demanded the right to vote.

Newspapers treated the convention as a joke, and even many abolitionists refused to take women's rights seriously. But while men laughed, women across the country established women's rights groups. More conventions and meetings followed the historic Seneca Falls Convention.

Up to the beginning of the Civil War, many women's rights activists also supported the abolitionist and temperance (anti-alcohol) movements. Their attitude changed when the war ended and the Fifteenth Amendment gave African Americans the right to vote. Some women's rights activists opposed passage of the amendment unless it included women. The issue split the movement into two factions: one focused on gaining the right to vote, the other on advocating for a

Today, the chapel that hosted the Seneca Falls Convention in 1848 and other sites related to the suffrage movement are part of the Women's Rights National Historical Park. These bronze statues depict Elizabeth Cady Stanton, Frederick Douglass, and Lucretia Mott, among others who attended the convention.

wider range of equal rights for women. The groups achieved significant progress—women gained the right to own property and sign contracts—but they were still denied the right to vote.

The two organizations merged in 1890 and continued agitating for the right to vote. Members of a new radical splinter group employed tactics such as hunger strikes and picketing. In 1920, the Nineteenth Amendment finally granted women the right to vote.

THE FEMINIST MOVEMENT

During the 1960s, a second wave of women's rights activism began as women pushed for equal rights in the workplace, social equality, and reproductive rights. In 1963, Betty Friedan's book *The Feminine Mystique* challenged women's roles as housewives. A report that year by the President's Commission on the Status of Women revealed pervasive sexism in every aspect of society, and President John F. Kennedy signed into law

Feminists march for their cause in 1977. The demonstrators include the great-niece of Susan B. Anthony *(left, in black top)*, U.S. Representative Bella Abzug *(in hat)*, and Betty Friedan *(in red coat)*.

the Equal Pay Act for women. In the Civil Rights Act of 1964, Congress included protections against discrimination against women in the workplace.

The Equal Employment Opportunity Commission (EEOC), set up by the 1964 act, demonstrated little interest in enforcing the provision on discrimination by sex. In response, Friedan and other feminists organized the National Organization for Women (NOW) in 1966. NOW protested EEOC policies and went on to champion a wide range of women's rights issues. Radical feminist groups also formed and organized unconventional and audacious demonstrations. Women's rights became a huge movement—in 1970, tens of thousands of women, including Friedan, feminist Gloria Steinem, and U.S. Representative Bella Abzug, marched in New York City for the Women's Strike for Equality.

Lawmakers responded with measures that granted affirmative action rights to women, prohibited discrimination against pregnant women, ensured women's access to banking and credit services, and promoted equality in schools. Title IX, a statute passed in 1972, transformed women's athletics by requiring equal treatment of women in education. Meanwhile, the Supreme Court struck down many laws that discriminated against women, such as exclusion from jury duty, or that set different standards between men and women, such as granting alimony to women but not to men.

Some of the most groundbreaking changes dealt with women's sexuality and reproductive rights. Oral contraceptives were made available in 1960, and in 1965, the Supreme Court ruled in the case of *Griswold v. Connecticut* that laws banning contraceptives were a violation of privacy. Title X of the Public Health Service Act of 1970 authorized grants for family planning and related health services. In 1973, the Supreme Court legalized abortion in the case of *Roe v.*

After the Supreme Court ruled that the Virginia Military Institute—the last all-male public university in the United States—must admit women, the first female cadets enrolled in 1997.

Wade, one of the most revolutionary and controversial court cases of the century.

One of the women's rights movement's highest priorities was the passage of the Equal Rights Amendment (ERA) to the U.S. Constitution. The wording of the proposed amendment had been introduced in Congress in 1923, and it was reintroduced and passed in both houses in 1972. To be adopted, it had to be approved by thirty-eight states. The ERA became the target of antifeminist organizations, however. It was passed only in thirty-five states, and in 1982, the deadline for ratification elapsed.

Nevertheless, the Supreme Court has upheld equal protection of the law for women in several landmark cases. In *Reed v. Reed* (1971), the Supreme Court struck down a law that men could not be given preference over women in being appointed to administer an estate. The verdict was narrowly applied to the specific case—it was not broad enough to invoke equal protection in other cases of discrimination. In 1996, the Court applied the strictest interpretation of equal protection in the case of *United States v. Virginia*. The suit was based on a complaint by a female high school student against the Virginia Military Institute, the state's only all-male public higher-education institution. The Court ruled that the school must admit women on the grounds of the equal protection guarantee in the Constitution.

THE LEGACY OF *ROE v. WADE*

In 1970, an unnamed pregnant woman, "Jane Roe," challenged a Texas law banning abortion except when the mother's life was in danger. She filed a federal lawsuit against Dallas County District Attorney Henry Wade, who represented the state of Texas. The Texas district court ruled in Roe's favor, and Wade appealed to the Supreme Court. In 1973, by a 7–2 margin, the Court found the Texas law unconstitutional on the grounds that it violated the Fourteenth Amendment, "which protects against state action the right to privacy, including a woman's qualified right to terminate her pregnancy."

Initially, the women's rights movement considered *Roe* a minor victory. The verdict could have been broader because the Court left open the option that less restrictive antiabortion laws could be considered constitutional.

In reaction to *Roe*, a number of states moved quickly to restrict access to abortion. There have been periodic challenges to the ruling ever since—some upheld, others struck down. The Court upheld the Hyde Amendment of 1976, which prohibited federal funding for abortions. Nevertheless, *Roe* stands as the definitive ruling on the issue of abortion.

ISSUES CONFRONTING WOMEN TODAY

Women's rights activism waned after the 1970s. Feminists experienced a backlash from conservative groups, and divisions emerged within the movement itself. The political and social climate of the nation also discouraged activism.

Nonetheless, issues concerning women's rights remain hot topics of debate in the twenty-first century. Opponents of abortion never accepted the *Roe v. Wade* verdict—if anything, the decision has grown even more divisive over the years. Republican lawmakers have vowed to overturn *Roe v. Wade*, with the party platform calling for a constitutional ban on abortion. The Supreme Court has revisited the topic of abortion, in many cases upholding laws restricting access to abortion. In *Gonzales v. Carhart* (2003), the Court upheld a ban passed by Congress on partial-birth abortion, even to protect the health of the mother.

Other reproductive rights issues have also proven to be controversial. The Patient Protection and Affordable Care Act of 2010 mandated that insurance plans cover birth control. Conservative lawmakers and some religious leaders protested the mandate on the grounds that it violated the freedom of people who opposed birth control for religious reasons.

Women have largely gained legal equality in the United States, but economic inequality persists. According to a report by the American Association of University Women, women earned on average 77 percent of men's earnings in 2010. Many factors contribute to the disparity—women are more likely to take a break from the workplace when they become mothers, for example, and some lower-paying fields are dominated by women—but pay discrimination is also a factor. Congress passed the Lilly Ledbetter Fair Pay Act in 2009 but failed in 2012 to approve the Paycheck Fairness Act, which would have strengthened antidiscrimination measures.

In the past, the so-called mommy wars were a debate between working women and stay-at-home mothers. Today, when most women work at some point while raising children, the term refers more often to the struggle to balance work and family. Some employers offer family-friendly policies such as flex time and generous paid parental leave, but many women don't have such options. In addition, paying for good-quality childcare is a huge hurdle for many families. Back in 1971, Congress passed the Comprehensive Child Development Act, which would have established federally funded childcare. President Richard Nixon vetoed the bill, however, and the idea has never been seriously revisited.

LGBT RIGHTS

CHAPTER 6

I n August 2012, musician Rufus Wainwright married Jorn Wiesbrodt in New York. The media reported on the star-studded list of attendees, the clothes worn by the happy couple, the music played during the ceremony, and the menu at the reception. Guests received jars of local plum jam. The fact that Wainwright was marrying another man was no big deal in the headlines.

The event illustrates the progress made by the gay rights movement since the late twentieth century. Throughout history, homosexuality was widely regarded as being abnormal. Gays and lesbians were subject to discrimination under the law and in their everyday lives. As recently as 1986, the Supreme Court ruling in the case of *Bowers v. Hardwick* upheld a state law that outlawed certain gay sexual practices. Few gays and lesbians were willing to come out of the closet, or make their sexuality publicly known. It could mean personal and professional disaster.

Today, numerous celebrities and public figures are openly gay and experience little public disapproval for their sexuality. Compared to other movements, the gay rights movement emerged recently and quickly made substantial progress. Today, it's often referred to as the lesbian, gay, bisexual, and transsexual, or LGBT, movement. Nevertheless, gays still lack significant legal rights in the United States, particularly when it comes to marriage equality and antidiscrimination laws.

The annual New York City Gay Pride March commemorates the Stonewall Riots of 1969. More than a million people of all sexual orientations line the streets each year to watch the parade.

THE RISE OF THE LGBT RIGHTS MOVEMENT

In 1969, New York City police launched a late-night raid on the gay bar Stonewall Inn. Police harassment of gay bars was common at the time. Instead of clearing out, though, the crowd outside began fighting back. The Stonewall Riots, as they're called, galvanized the emerging gay rights movement and focused national attention on the issue of gay rights. Before Stonewall, many Americans would have been doubtful of the very concept of gay rights. A year later, the first gay pride parade made its way down the streets of New York.

The 1970s saw some legislative and legal progress for gay rights. In 1977, though, anti-gay activists campaigned to repeal an anti-discriminatory ordinance in Dade County, Florida, one of the first such laws in the country. The ordinance was revoked by a wide margin. Also in 1977, however, Harvey Milk, the city supervisor of San Francisco, California, became the first openly gay public official.

Despite public opposition in some areas to pro-gay legislation, the Supreme Court expanded gay rights in several landmark court cases. In *Romer v. Evans* (1996), the Court struck down an extreme provision in the Colorado constitution that denied gays equal

In 2004, after the legalization of gay marriage in Massachusetts, this same-sex couple became the first in that state to exchange wedding vows.

protection of the law. In *Lawrence v. Texas* (2003), the Court struck down a law prohibiting certain gay sexual practices, overruling the earlier *Bowers* verdict. It found that such laws violated due process and mentioned the right to privacy.

In 1996, President Bill Clinton signed into law the Defense of Marriage Act (DOMA), which prohibited federal recognition of same-sex unions. Alaska became the first state to ban gay marriage in 1998, and it was followed by many others. Nevertheless, DOMA and anti-gay laws did not put an end to LGBT hopes of gaining the right to marry. Some states began recognizing civil unions, which gave gays many of the same legal rights as marriage. In 2004, Massachusetts became the first state to legalize gay marriage. In 2012, President Barack Obama became the first U.S. president to publicly endorse same-sex marriage.

"Don't Ask, Don't Tell"

Meanwhile, policy concerning gays serving in the military had become a national issue. The military had long prohibited gays from service. If a service member was revealed to be gay, he or she was discharged.

In 1993, President Clinton made a reversal of the ban one of his early priorities in office. He encountered intense resistance from military commanders and the general public. He negotiated a compromise in the "Policy on Homosexual Conduct in the Armed Forces," which initiated the "Don't ask, don't tell" era in the military. Gays could serve in the armed forces as long as they concealed their sexuality. The Clinton administration represented the issue as a matter of personal privacy. To many gays in the military, "Don't ask, don't tell" violated their personal integrity by forcing them to conceal their sexual identity.

President Obama opposed "Don't ask, don't tell" and began considering a repeal after taking office. He approached the issue carefully because he did not want to create a disruption while the military was

A woman holds a sign supporting the end of the "Don't ask, don't tell" policy in 2011. A year after that policy ended, studies found that the repeal had no negative effects on military readiness or morale.

involved in two wars. In 2010, he announced that he was planning to work for a repeal of the policy. Several top military officials agreed that gays should be permitted to serve openly.

The courts were also moving toward the legal rejection of "Don't ask, don't tell." In 2010, a federal judge ruled it unconstitutional and a violation of service members' rights. The judge stated that the government failed to make a convincing case that the policy served the best interests of the military. The ruling was upheld in a higher court.

Congress approved legislation repealing "Don't ask, don't tell" in late 2010. Implementation of the repeal began in late 2011. As reported in the *New York Times*, more than thirteen thousand gay service members had been discharged during the eighteen years that "Don't ask, don't tell" was in effect.

LGBT ISSUES TODAY

In the twenty-first century, gays continue to fight for equal rights. Laws in many states and cities still discriminate against LGBT people or fail to provide equal protection. Gays lack many equal rights concerning marriage equality, adoption, and discrimination in the workplace and other areas. In 2007, the House of Representatives passed a bill prohibiting employment discrimination based on sexual orientation, but the Senate did not approve it. In 2009,

President Obama signed into law a Hate Crimes Prevention Act that gave federal authorities the means to prosecute crimes based on the victim's sexual identity.

The DOMA remains in effect, barring federal recognition of gay marriage. The Obama administration has officially refused to defend it, however, and the Democratic Party embraces marriage equality in its party platform. In the states, gay marriage and civil unions have seen both progress and setbacks. In California, in 2008, the courts ruled in favor of gay

"It Gets Better"

In September 2010, gay columnist Dan Savage and his partner posted a video on YouTube with a simple message for LGBT adolescents: "It gets better." Savage was reacting to several recent suicides by gay youths who had been bullied by their peers. He wanted to tell LGBT teens that they're not alone, that their difficult high school years wouldn't last forever, and that they could get through it.

Later in September, Rutgers University student Tyler Clementi committed suicide after his roommate secretly taped Clementi's sexual encounter with another man. The tragedy stunned Americans across the country. Many were inspired to add their own stories to Savage's It Gets Better Project, which became a worldwide movement. Within a couple of years, the number of videos posted increased to the tens of thousands. They include entries from celebrities and ordinary individuals and represent all sexual orientations.

marriage, only to have voters reject recognition of gay marriages in a ballot measure.

In recent years, gay rights activism has expanded to include the rights of transsexuals, also called the transgendered. Transsexuals are people who identify psychologically as members of the opposite sex. Some choose to reassign their legal gender on driver's licenses and birth certificates, which is legal in most states. Transsexuals are protected under the Hate Crimes Protection Act of 2009, and court cases have granted transsexuals federal antidiscrimination protection in

Demonstrators hold banners at a transgender rights rally. In many states, transgender people experience discrimination yet lack equal protection under the law.

the workplace. Nonetheless, transgendered individuals still lack broad equal protection of the law.

Public opinion has shifted to largely support LGBT rights. In 1997, entertainer Ellen DeGeneres revealed that she was a lesbian, prompting a frenzy of controversy in the media and condemnation by conservative groups. The revelation negatively affected her career, leaving DeGeneres in a deep depression for several years. More recently, gay public figures and celebrities have experienced little backlash on revealing their sexual orientation. CNN anchor Anderson Cooper stated in mid-2012 that he was gay. Also in 2012, rapper Frank Ocean revealed that his first love was another man, marking a milestone for the often anti-gay hip-hop genre.

THE EXPANSION OF EQUAL RIGHTS

S ince the founding of the United States, and particularly since the civil rights era of the middle twentieth century, policymakers and ordinary Americans alike have grown more receptive to the diverse needs of some groups within society. In some cases, expanding equal rights has required difficult decisions. Do prisoners and illegal immigrants deserve equal protection under the law? Is it constitutional to forbid religious practices that are in conflict with the law? What rights should be accorded to developmentally disabled adults who may not be capable of living independently? In general, legislators and the courts have moved to make equal rights possible for all Americans, not just the majority.

THE RIGHTS OF MINORS

When people discuss "children's rights," they are usually referring to the basic requirements for their general welfare. Children have the right to food and health care, a home, and education. They have a right to grow up without experiencing abuse or neglect.

Christopher Simmons was placed on death row in Missouri for killing a woman when he was seventeen years old. The Supreme Court overturned his death sentence in 2005.

The first laws concerning the legal rights of children were passed in the early twentieth century, when child labor was outlawed. Legal protections for children were developed slowly because many people held that government intrusion interfered with parents' discipline and constituted a privacy violation. In 1962, the amended Social Security Act included provisions for child welfare and protection. The Child Abuse Prevention and Treatment Act of 1974 created services for handling cases of child abuse and neglect.

A juvenile justice system separate from the adult criminal justice system deals with young offenders. Many of the court procedures are similar in the two systems, but the juvenile

In re Gault (1967) and the Juvenile Justice System

The U.S. juvenile justice system was founded in the nineteenth century on the concept of *parens patriae*, the "parent of the country" philosophy. It held that it was the duty of the government to act in the best interest of juvenile offenders and serve as their protective guardian. Hearings in juvenile courts were informal, with few strict procedures.

In 1967, the Supreme Court ruling on the case of *In re Gault* brought drastic changes to the juvenile justice system. Three years earlier, fifteen-year-old Gerald Gault (who was already serving probation for a prior offense) had been taken into custody for allegedly making an obscene phone call to a neighbor. His parents, who were at work, were not informed of his detention and court appearance, and the neighbor never appeared to testify. Gault was found delinquent and committed to the state reform school until the age of twenty-one. He appealed the case, and eventually the Court overturned the conviction, ruling that juveniles facing institutional confinement—the juvenile equivalent of jail time—are entitled to certain constitutional rights, including the right to an attorney.

The *Gault* case granted juvenile offenders many of the same legal rights as adult criminals, which led to juvenile court hearings becoming more similar to criminal court proceedings.

court focuses on rehabilitation of youths rather than punishment. In addition, the juvenile justice system recognizes that young offenders lack adult maturity and judgment. In the case of *Roper v. Simmons*

(2005), the Supreme Court abolished the death penalty for offenders who were under the age of eighteen at the time of the crime, partially because of juveniles' psychological differences from adults.

THE RIGHTS OF OLDER AMERICANS

Discrimination on the basis of age is prohibited by the Fourteenth Amendment and outlawed in the workplace in the 1967 Age Discrimination in Employment Act. Nonetheless, age discrimination has become an issue of concern in the twenty-first century, as baby boomers—those born between 1946 and 1965—grow older. In a tough economic climate, many in this age group want to work past the traditional age of retirement, even as jobs have become harder to find and keep. The number of age discrimination complaints filed by older Americans has been increasing year after year. Unfortunately for older adults, age discrimination is extremely difficult to prove. In *Gross v. FBL Financial Services, Inc.* (2009), the Supreme Court imposed a higher burden of proof for age discrimination cases than for cases involving race or gender.

Elderly Americans can be vulnerable to abuse or neglect by caregivers or criminals. Abuse may involve physical or emotional mistreatment by a caregiver or financial abuse, such as theft or misuse of power of

Demonstrators gather in Washington, D.C., in 2008 to support the Community Choice Act, which grants people who have disabilities alternatives to nursing homes and other institutions.

attorney. State laws offer adult protective services for victims of abuse, although specific provisions vary from state to state.

THE RIGHTS OF PEOPLE WHO ARE DISABLED

Historically, disabled Americans have been subject to discrimination and denial of equal rights. In many cases, physical disabilities meant that people were unable to access public buildings or use public transportation. Policies regarding disabled Americans were often restrictive and marginalizing—some states prohibited people with certain disabilities from showing themselves in public.

In the 1960s, activists began campaigning for expanded rights that would allow people with disabilities to participate more fully in society. Laws were passed that required employers to make workplaces handicap-accessible, prohibited employment discrimination, and granted educational rights to disabled students. The greatest victory for people who were disabled came in 1990 with the passage of the Americans with Disabilities Act, which required equal treatment and equal access across a broad range of public places and services.

People with intellectual and development disorders, as well as those with mental illnesses, also face discrimination in work and daily life. In the past, many of these individuals were confined to huge institutions. Supreme Court cases such as *Olmstead v. L.C.* (1999) ruled that people with mental disabilities must be allowed to live in regular communities rather than institutions, if medically possible. In 2000, the Developmental Disabilities Assistance and Bill of Rights Act was passed to improve community-based services for people who have development disabilities.

Since the 1990s, rates of autism, a developmental disorder, have surged. As these autistic children reach adulthood, their rights and needs will become a more pressing issue.

THE RIGHTS OF PRISONERS

Even when they are imprisoned for breaking the law, Americans retain some basic rights. They are granted a basic standard of living by the constitutional prohibition of cruel and unusual punishment. Prisoners retain some rights to free speech and religious practice, and they can possess certain personal items. The law requires that they have access to an attorney and the courts. Specific rights and restrictions vary from state to state.

In the 1960s, terrible conditions in prisons led to reforms and the establishment of certain rights for prisoners. Nonetheless, conditions in some prisons today are inhumane and overcrowded.

Once prisoners are released, their rights may still be restricted by a state's civil disability laws regarding former offenders. They may be barred from holding political office or serving on a jury. Some former offenders lose their occupational licenses, meaning that they will not be able to practice their former trade upon release. In many states, former sex offenders must report personal information so that they can be tracked on a sex offender registry.

The right to vote may be restricted for convicts, parolees, and ex-offenders. Laws vary from state to state.

THE RIGHTS OF IMMIGRANTS

Excepting Native Americans and early African Americans, every U.S. citizen is here as a result of immigration. Nonetheless, each new wave of immigrants has met with hostility from established Americans. The Irish were subjected to belittlement and job discrimination when they arrived in the mid-nineteenth century, as were the Chinese and Japanese and Eastern European immigrants who arrived in the early twentieth century. The tendency continues today with discrimination against Hispanic immigrants.

Anti-immigrant groups have periodically started their own activist movements in the United States. During the 1850s, the "Know Nothings" campaigned on a political platform of immigration restriction and limiting the influence of immigrants. In 2005, a civilian group calling itself the Minuteman Project organized to patrol the U.S.-Mexican border for illegal immigrants.

Immigrants, both legal and illegal, are entitled to the liberties listed in the Bill of Rights of the U.S. Constitution. Discrimination based on race or national origin is prohibited. Illegal immigrants facing deportation are granted certain due process rights, such as the right to a hearing and legal representation.

An immigrants rights coalition holds a rally in response to the 2012 ruling on Arizona's harsh immigration law. The Supreme Court struck down three provisions but upheld the fourth.

Illegal immigrants are not guaranteed full protection under U.S. laws, however.

RIGHTS OF RELIGIOUS GROUPS

In colonial times, many settlers fled their home countries and came to America to escape religious persecution. The framers of the Constitution believed that the government should neither promote nor suppress religious practices. The right to freedom of religion is preserved for all Americans in the First Amendment. The Fourteenth Amendment is also interpreted to protect against discrimination based on religious belief.

Religious practices spark controversy, however, when they come into conflict with the law. As seen earlier, some religious groups have objected to being required by law to include contraceptives in employee health care packages. The Supreme Court has upheld the freedom of religious expression in cases arguing that Amish children should not be required to attend high school, that religious canvassing is legal, and that Seventh-Day Adventists can collect unemployment benefits even if they refuse to work on the Sabbath. It has rejected arguments for Mormon polygamy; wearing religious symbols while in military uniform; and a challenge of a state law banning peyote, a hallucinogenic drug used in Native American religious ceremonies. The Court has also struck down cases on matters that violated the separation of church and state, such as requiring prayer in public schools.

Throughout American history, people have sometimes become the target of discrimination because of their religion. In the past, Catholics and Jews were victims of religious discrimination. More recently, Muslims have experienced discrimination after the 9/11 terrorist attacks in the United States. Anti-Muslim crimes increased drastically in 2001 following these attacks.

CHAPTER 8

THE FUTURE OF
EQUAL RIGHTS

The civil rights era opened up previously unimagined opportunities for tens of millions of American citizens. The election of Barack Obama, the first African American president, provided proof that there really was no limit to how much a member of a minority group could accomplish. Occasionally, however, instances of injustice occur that remind everyone of the fragility of some of their rights. The fight for equal rights is not over. It's important that people continue to defend personal liberties.

In the early twenty-first century, yet another type of inequality emerged as a major issue. The income disparity between wealthy and poor Americans was increasing dramatically, and many experts worry that it could eventually impact social and economic stability.

ECONOMIC INEQUALITY

Following the financial crisis of 2008, many average Americans lost their jobs or saw their incomes drop. They lost their homes and their savings. The cost of higher education

Occupy Wall Street protesters in New York demonstrate against bank bailouts, foreclosures, high unemployment, and a range of other issues.

soared, putting a good-quality education out of reach for many young people and burdening others with student loan debt. Meanwhile, corporate profits quickly rebounded and the richest Americans grew richer.

The aftermath of the recession sparked a debate over economic injustices in the country. A new movement, Occupy Wall Street, briefly gained national prominence. Historically, most protest movements have championed the rights of minorities. Occupy Wall Street, however, claimed to represent the 99 percent, meaning that it spoke for the economic interests of all but the wealthiest Americans. Since the 1980s, income inequality has been increasing. The gap has grown more sharply since the beginning of the twenty-first century. In 2011, the percentage of Americans living below the poverty line was 15 percent, according to the U.S. Census Bureau.

Contrary to some assertions, however, economic equality has never been a right granted to all Americans. Ideally, increased civil rights create equal opportunities that result in economic progress for oppressed minorities. As Federal Reserve Chairman Ben Bernanke said in a 2007 speech, "Although we Americans strive to provide equality of economic opportunity, we do not guarantee equality of economic outcomes, nor should we." Today, most Americans are accorded rights that should enable them to succeed and attain the American dream.

Nonetheless, many people are not benefiting from the opportunities made possible by these rights. In the past, economic disparities were greatest between the majority and various minorities. Recently, the ranks of Americans falling behind in income do not correlate to gender, race, ethnicity, or other minority categories. The number of middle-class Americans has diminished. Income among members of the middle class declined slightly during the 2000s, and the wealth of the middle class decreased sharply. A 2012 Pew Research Center report described the rise in residential segregation by income since 1980, meaning that more people are living in neighborhoods that are either chiefly wealthy or poor.

A majority of Americans were affected by the recession, but minority groups experienced worse hardship. Prior to the financial meltdown, members of minority groups were disproportionately steered to home loans known as subprime mortgages. More people than ever before achieved the dream of owning their own home, but the deceptive terms of the loans made it difficult for them to make payments. Many of these owners lost their homes and their investments when home prices plummeted. In addition, the economic recovery occurred more slowly for members of minority groups. Unemployment levels remained much higher for African Americans and Hispanics than for other Americans. More men than women lost their jobs during the recession, but during the recovery, more men gained jobs than women did.

The growing income disparity is a matter of great concern to economists, public officials, and ordinary Americans. But even though it is an issue involving inequality, it is not strictly a rights issue. If the government took action to address income disparity, it would probably require a combination of social policy—such as improving the quality and accessibility of education—and economic policy, such as enacting measures that would increase hiring.

RIGHTS OF SERVICE MEMBERS AND VETERANS

Service members in the armed forces are protected by most of the provisions in the Bill of Rights. In some cases, however, free speech is curtailed in the interest of national security and discipline within ranks. The Uniform Code of Military Justice restricts free speech in several articles. In addition, service members are required to obey the orders of their commanders, even if the orders limit free speech. In the early twenty-first century, soldiers' blogs became a controversial free speech issue.

Servicewomen are subject to another, more damaging suppression of rights: high rates of sexual assault with inadequate support for victims. They are discouraged from reporting instances of rape, and few attackers are disciplined.

Military veterans returning from active duty are granted certain special rights. The Uniformed Services Employment and Reemployment Rights Act of 1994 guarantees that veterans can return to their civilian jobs upon leaving military service. Veterans may also qualify for health benefits, educational assistance, and home loan guarantees.

THE ONGOING STRUGGLE FOR EQUALITY

In 2012, many of the controversial news stories that engaged the public and emerged as issues in the campaign for U.S. president involved equal rights. The media reported, for example, on gay marriage, immigration, and women's reproductive rights. All of these issues continue to be matters of debate and legal action in the effort to preserve and expand equal rights for every American.

Today, the biggest fight in women's rights is to hang onto the reproductive rights victories achieved in years past. Women have recently seen some of these rights come under attack. They also continue to receive lower average pay than men and still

Reproductive rights activists hold a "Stand up for Women's Health" rally in Washington, D.C., to oppose government defunding of Planned Parenthood.

pull off the difficult task of balancing work and family life.

Gay rights activists are focused on the next step in achieving marriage equality. In California, gay marriage advocates are preparing to take the appeal against Proposition 8 to the U.S. Supreme Court.

Congress has made no progress in recent years on reforming immigration law. The 2012 Deferred Action for Childhood Arrivals initiative provides temporary security for some young immigrants, but it does not offer a long-term solution.

The state of public schools is another issue of concern. Education is a basic right for all Americans, but today, not all public schools provide a high-quality education. Minority students, in particular, are more likely to struggle in school and are less likely to graduate. One contributing factor to the "education gap" is that low-income school districts, which are more likely to have a large number of minority students, lack the educational resources of richer school districts. Charter schools have arisen as an alternative to traditional public schools, but critics maintain that they merely divert money away from the public school system and that charter school students do not perform any better academically.

Civil rights groups have denounced New York's "stop and frisk" police practices. Here, a youth organizer demonstrates a smartphone app that monitors stop and frisk police action.

African Americans and other racial minorities continue to struggle against discrimination. For example, the discriminatory practice of racial profiling by law enforcement has been a huge issue. Today, the "stop and frisk" policy in New York City has revisited the debate. Police can detain and pat down people on the street if they have reason to suspect criminal activity. An overwhelming proportion of the people subjected to stop and frisk are minorities, however, and the police have been harshly criticized for using race rather than reasonable suspicion as a criterion.

THE BILL OF RIGHTS

PREAMBLE TO THE CONSTITUTION

We the People of the United States, in order to form a more perfect Union, establish Justice, insure domestic Tranquility, provide for the common defense, promote the general Welfare, and secure the Blessings of Liberty to ourselves and our Posterity, do ordain and establish this Constitution for the United States of America.

On September 25, 1789, Congress transmitted to the state legislatures twelve proposed amendments, two of which, having to do with congressional representation and congressional pay, were not adopted. The remaining ten amendments became the Bill of Rights.

THE BILL OF RIGHTS

Amendment I

Congress shall make no law respecting an establishment of religion, or prohibiting the free exercise thereof; or abridging the freedom of speech, or of the press; or the right of the people peaceably to assemble, and to petition the Government for a redress of grievances.

THE BILL OF RIGHTS

Amendment II

A well regulated Militia, being necessary to the security of a free State, the right of the people to keep and bear Arms, shall not be infringed.

Amendment III

No Soldier shall, in time of peace be quartered in any house, without the consent of the Owner, nor in time of war, but in a manner to be prescribed by law.

Amendment IV

The right of the people to be secure in their persons, houses, papers, and effects, against unreasonable searches and seizures, shall not be violated, and no Warrants shall issue, but upon probable cause, supported by Oath or affirmation, and particularly describing the place to be searched, and the persons or things to be seized.

Amendment V

No person shall be held to answer for a capital, or otherwise infamous crime, unless on a presentment or indictment of a Grand Jury, except in cases arising in the land or naval forces, or in the Militia, when in actual service in time of War or public danger; nor shall any person be subject for the same offence to be twice put in jeopardy of life or limb; nor shall be compelled in any criminal case to be a witness against himself, nor be deprived of life, liberty, or property, without due process of law; nor shall private property be taken for public use, without just compensation.

Amendment VI

In all criminal prosecutions, the accused shall enjoy the right to a speedy and public trial, by an impartial jury of the State and district wherein the crime shall have been committed, which district shall have been previously ascertained by law, and to be informed of the nature and cause of the accusation; to be confronted with the witnesses against him; to have compulsory process for obtaining witnesses in his favor, and to have the Assistance of Counsel for his defense.

Amendment VII

In Suits at common law, where the value in controversy shall exceed twenty dollars, the right of trial by jury shall be preserved, and no fact tried by a jury, shall be otherwise reexamined in any Court of the United States, than according to the rules of the common law.

Amendment VIII

Excessive bail shall not be required, nor excessive fines imposed, nor cruel and unusual punishments inflicted.

Amendment IX

The enumeration in the Constitution, of certain rights, shall not be construed to deny or disparage others retained by the people.

Amendment X

The powers not delegated to the United States by the Constitution, nor prohibited by it to the States, are reserved to the States respectively, or to the people.

act A law or statute passed by a legislative body.

activism Direct involvement in a cause with the goal of achieving political or social change.

affirmative action A policy of promoting rights and equal opportunities for members of groups who have historically been disenfranchised.

amendment A change of or addition to a document such as a bill or constitution.

appeal To apply for the transfer of a case to a higher court for a new hearing.

assimilation The absorption and integration of people, ideas, or culture into a wider society or culture.

audacious Displaying a willingness to take surprisingly bold risks.

Bill of Rights The first ten amendments added to the U.S. Constitution in 1791 that protect basic rights and liberties.

boycott A protest in which people refuse to buy or use a product or service.

case A legal dispute that is heard in a court of law.

charter school A publicly funded elementary or secondary school that is exempted from some rules, regulations, and statutes that apply to other public schools in exchange for agreeing to meet certain performance standards as stipulated in the school's charter.

civil liberties Principles of law that grant rights to citizens and limit government powers.

civil union A legally recognized relationship, usually between a same-sex couple, that grants many of the rights of marriage.

contraceptive A device or drug that prevents pregnancy.

discrimination Prejudicial treatment of members of a certain group because of their age, class, religion, race, gender, sexual orientation, disability, or other such characteristic.

due process Fair treatment under the law.

Equal Protection Clause The section of the Fourteenth Amendment to the U.S. Constitution that prohibits discrimination by state government institutions.

explicit Stated clearly and in detail so that there is no room for doubt.

intern To confine as a prisoner.

oppress To subject to harsh or unfair treatment.

privacy The right to be left alone from interference by the government or other people.

racism The belief that one race is inherently superior than another race or that certain races are inherently inferior.

ratification The act of confirming by approval or consent, such as to a treaty or contract.

repeal To officially revoke, such as a law or official policy.

reservation Land granted to Native Americans by Congress or by treaty.

segregation The enforced separation of members of different groups, such as by race.

treaty A formal agreement between two or more nations, states, or sovereign powers, including Native American tribes.

U.S. Supreme Court The highest court in the nation's judicial system.

American Civil Liberties Union (ACLU)
125 Broad Street, 18th Floor
New York, NY 10004
(212) 549-2500
Web site: http://www.aclu.org
The ACLU works to protect liberty and defends individual rights
    and liberties that the U.S. Constitution and laws of the
    United States guarantee everyone in the nation.

American Constitution Society for Law and Policy
1333 H Street NW, 11th Floor
Washington, DC 20005
(202) 393-6181
Web site: http://www.acslaw.org
The American Constitution Society for Law and Policy promotes
    the vitality of the U.S. Constitution and the fundamental
    values it expresses.

Bill of Rights Institute
200 North Glebe Road, Suite 200
Arlington, VA 22203
(703) 894-1776
Web site: http://www.billofrightsinstitute.org
The Bill of Rights Institute's mission is to educate young people
    about the words and ideas of America's founders, the liber-
    ties guaranteed in founding documents, and the continued
    impact of those principles.

Canadian Bar Association (CBA)
500–865 Carling Avenue

Ottawa, ON K1S 5S8
Canada
(613) 237-2925
Web site: http://www.cba.org
The Canadian Bar Association is an organization made up of
members of Canada's legal profession.

Canadian Civil Liberties Association (CCLA)
506–360 Bloor Street West
Toronto, ON M5S 1X1
Canada
(416) 363-0321
Web site: http://ccla.org
The CCLA is a national organization that was constituted to promote respect for and observance of fundamental human
rights and civil liberties and to defend, extend, and foster recognition of these rights and liberties.

**National Association for the Advancement of Colored
People (NAACP)**
4805 Mount Hope Drive
Baltimore, MD 21215
(877) NAACP-98 [622-2798]
Web site: http://www.naacp.org
The mission of the NAACP is to ensure the political, educational,
social, and economic equality of rights of all people and to
eliminate race-based discrimination.

National Organization for Women (NOW)
1100 H Street NW, 3rd Floor

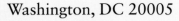

Washington, DC 20005

(202) 628-8669

Web site: http://www.now.org

NOW is the largest U.S. organization of feminist activists and works to bring about equality for all women.

Native American Rights Fund (NARF)

1506 Broadway

Boulder, CO 80302-6296

(303) 447-8760

Web site: http://www.narf.org

This nonprofit organization provides legal representation and technical assistance to Indian tribes, organizations, and individuals across the United States.

U.S. Commission on Civil Rights

624 Ninth Street NW

Washington, DC 20425

(202) 376-7700

Web site: http://www.usccr.gov

This agency investigates complaints about citizens being deprived of their right to vote by reason of their race, color, religion, sex, age, disability, or national origin or by reason of fraudulent practices.

U.S. Equal Employment Opportunity Commission (EEOC)

131 M Street NE

Washington, DC 20507

(202) 663-4900

Web site: http://www.eeoc.gov

The EEOC enforces federal laws that make it illegal to discriminate against a job applicant or employee because of a person's race, color, religion, sex, national origin, age (forty or older), disability, or genetic information.

U.S. National Archives and Records Administration (NARA)

8601 Adelphi Road

College Park, MD 20740

(866) 272-6272

Web site: http://www.archives.gov

The National Archives and Records Administration preserves government documents and records that have historical or legal significance.

WEB SITES

Due to the changing nature of Internet links, Rosen Publishing has developed an online list of Web sites related to the subject of this book. This site is updated regularly. Please use this link to access the list:

http://www.rosenlinks.com/pfcd/equal

Darraj, Susan Muaddi. *The Universal Declaration of Human Rights* (Milestones in Modern World History). New York, NY: Chelsea House Publishers, 2010.

Finkelman, Paul, ed. *Milestone Documents in American History: Exploring the Primary Sources That Shaped America*. Dallas, TX: Schlager Group, 2008.

Friedman, Lauri S. *Women's Rights* (Introducing Issues with Opposing Viewpoints). Farmington Hills, MI: Greenhaven Press, 2009.

Gorman, Jacqueline Laks. *The Modern Feminist Movement: Sisters Under the Skin, 1961–1979*. New York, NY: Chelsea House Publishers, 2011.

Graham, Amy. *A Look at the Bill of Rights: Protecting the Rights of Americans*. Berkeley Heights, NJ: Enslow Publishers, 2008.

Hall, Kermit, ed. *The Oxford Guide to United States Supreme Court Decisions*. 2nd ed. New York, NY: Oxford University Press, 2009.

Hasday, Judy L. *The Civil Rights Act of 1964* (Milestones in American History). New York, NY: Chelsea House Publishers, 2007.

Hennessey, Jonathan. *The United States Constitution: A Graphic Adaptation*. New York, NY: Hill and Wang, 2008.

Herda, D. J. *The Dred Scott Case* (Slavery and Citizenship). Rev. ed. Berkeley Heights, NJ: Enslow Publishers, 2010.

FOR FURTHER READING

Jacobs, Thomas A. *What Are My Rights?: Q & A About Teens and the Law.* Minneapolis, MN: Free Spirit Publishing, 2011.

Kallen, Stuart A. *Twentieth Century Immigration to the United States* (American History). Farmington Hills, MI: Lucent, 2007.

Kuhn, Betsy. *Gay Power! The Stonewall Riots and the Gay Rights Movement, 1969* (Civil Rights Struggles Around the World). Minneapolis, MN: Twenty-First Century Books, 2011.

Kukathas, Uma. *Native American Rights* (Issues on Trial). Farmington Hills, MI: Gale, 2008.

Miller, Debra A. *Immigration* (Current Controversies). Farmington Hills, MI: Greenhaven Press, 2010.

Ochoa, George, and Carter Smith. *Atlas of Hispanic-American History.* New York, NY: Facts On File, 2008.

Pederson, Charles E. *The U.S. Constitution and Bill of Rights.* Edina, MN: ABDO Publishing, 2010.

Savage, Dan, and Terry Miller. *It Gets Better: Coming Out, Overcoming Bullying, and Creating a Life Worth Living.* New York, NY: Dutton, 2011.

Uschan, Michael V. *The Civil Rights Movement* (American History). Farmington Hills, MI: Gale, 2010.

Alsenas, Linas. *Gay America: Struggle for Equality.* New York, NY: Amulet Books, 2008.

American Association of University Women. "The Simple Truth About the Gender Pay Gap." 2012. Retrieved August 31, 2012 (http://www.aauw.org /learn/research/upload/simpletruthaboutpaygap1.pdf).

Bernanke, Ben S. "The Level and Distribution of Economic Well-Being." Speech before the Greater Omaha Chamber of Commerce, Omaha, Nebraska, February 6, 2007. Retrieved August 31, 2012 (http://www.federalreserve.gov/newsevents /speech/bernanke20070206a.htm).

Boxer, Andrew. "Native Americans and the Federal Government." *History Today*, 2009. Retrieved August 31, 2012 (http://www.historytoday.com/ andrew-boxer/native-americans-and-federal -government).

Bravin, Jess, and Tamara Audi. "Court Splits on Arizona Law: Justices Rein in Law Aimed at Curbing Illegal Immigrants but Allow Police Checks." *Wall Street Journal*, June 25, 2012. Retrieved August 31, 2012 (http://online.wsj.com /article/SB10001424052702304898704577448039 2205316110.htm).

Brick, Kate, A. E. Challinor, and Marc R. Rosenblum. *Mexican and Central American Immigrants in the United States.* Washington, D.C.: Migration

Policy Institute, June 2011. Retrieved August 31, 2012 (http://www.migrationpolicy.org/pubs /MexCentAmimmigrants.pdf).

Clapham, Andrew. *Human Rights: A Very Short Introduction*. New York, NY: Oxford University Press, 2007.

Collins, Gail. *America's Women: Four Hundred Years of Dolls, Drudges, Helpmates, and Heroines*. New York, NY: William Morrow, 2003.

Cushman, Clare, ed. "Supreme Court Decisions and Women's Rights: Milestones to Equality." Supreme Court Historical Society, 2000. Retrieved August 31, 2012 (http://web.archive.org/web/200703 10085816/http://www.supremecourthistory.org /05_learning/subs/05_e.html).

"Don't Ask, Don't Tell." *New York Times*, September 20, 2011. Retrieved August 31, 2012 (http://topics .nytimes.com/top/reference/timestopics/subjects /d/dont_ask_dont_tell/index.html).

Fry, Richard, and Paul Taylor. "The Rise of Residential Segregation by Income." Pew Research Center, August 1, 2012. Retrieved August 31, 2012 (http://www.pewsocialtrends.org/2012/08/01 /the-rise-of-residential-segregation-by-income).

Harrison, Maureen, and Steve Gilbert, ed. *Civil Rights Decisions of the United States Supreme Court: The 19th Century*. Beverly Hills, CA: Excellent Books, 1994.

Knickerbocker, Brad. "Poll: Trayvon Martin Case Divides US by Race, Age, Wealth, and Politics." *Christian Science Monitor*, April 6, 2012. Retrieved August 31, 2012 (http://www.csmonitor .com/USA/Justice/2012/0406/Poll-Trayvon-Martin -case-divides-US-by-race-age-wealth-and-politics).

Kochhar, Rakesh. *The Demographics of the Jobs Recovery: Employment Gains by Race, Ethnicity, Gender and Nativity*. Pew Research Center, March 21, 2012. Retrieved August 31, 2012 (http:// pewresearch.org/pubs/2225/workforce -employment-hispanics-whites-blacks-asians -immigrants).

Kochhar, Rakesh, Richard Fry, and Paul Taylor. "Wealth Gaps Rise to Record Highs Between Whites, Blacks and Hispanics." Pew Research Center, July 26, 2011. Retrieved August 31, 2012 (http://pewresearch.org/pubs/2069/housing -bubble-subprime-mortgages-hispanics-blacks -household-wealth-disparity).

Levine, Michael L. *African Americans and Civil Rights: From 1619 to the Present*. Phoenix, AZ: Oryx Press, 1996.

Mendoza, Nadia. "Raise Your Glasses! Rufus Wainwright Weds Jorn Weisbrodt After Five Years Together...as Transgender Artist Conducts Ceremony." *Daily Mail*, August 24, 2012.

Retrieved August 31, 2012 (http://www.dailymail
.co.uk/tvshowbiz/article-2193220/Rufus
-Wainwright-weds-Jorn-Weisbrodt-years
---transgender-artist-conducts-ceremony.html).

Savage, David G. *The Supreme Court and Individual
Rights*. 5th ed. Washington, D.C.: CQ Press, 2009.

Sigler, Jay A. *Civil Rights in America: 1500 to the
Present*. Detroit, MI: Gale, 1998.

Stansell, Christine. *The Feminist Promise: 1792 to the
Present*. New York, NY: Modern Library, 2010.

"Stop-and-Frisk in New York City." *New York Times*,
August 8, 2012. Retrieved August 31, 2012 (http://
www.nytimes.com/2012/08/09/opinion/stop-and
-frisk-in-new-york-city.html).

Taylor, Paul, ed. "The Lost Decade of the Middle
Class: Fewer, Poorer, Gloomier." Pew Research
Center, August 22, 2012. Retrieved August 31,
2012 (http://www.pewsocialtrends.org/2012/08
/22/the-lost-decade-of-the-middle-class).

Taylor, Paul, ed. "The Rise of Asian Americans." Pew
Research Center, June 19, 2012. Retrieved August
31, 2012 (http://www.pewsocialtrends.org/2012
/06/19/the-rise-of-asian-americans).

ABOUT THE AUTHOR

Corona Brezina has written more than a dozen books for young adults. Several of her previous books have also focused on issues related to civil rights and the law, including *Amendments to the Constitution: The Fifth Amendment* and *FAQ Teen Life: Frequently Asked Questions About Juvenile Detention*. She lives in Chicago, Illinois.

PHOTO CREDITS

Cover, pp. 1, 3, 7, 16, 27, 36, 38, 49, 59, 64, 69, 82 Justin Sullivan/ Getty Images; pp. 4, 47, 54, 79, 89 © AP Images; pp. 8, 74–75 Chip Somodevilla/Getty Images; p. 11 Arizona State Library, Archives and Public Records, History and Archives Division, Phoenix, 00-0517; p. 14 Fotosearch/Archive Photos/Getty Images; p. 18 Library of Congress Manuscript Division; p. 22 Mario Tama/Getty Images; p. 25 Underwood Archives/Archive Photos/ Getty Images; p. 29 MPI/ Archive Photos/Getty Images; p. 31 Pictorial Parade/Archive Photos/Getty Images; p. 34 Francis Miller/Time & Life Pictures/Getty Images; p. 39 Dorothea Lange/ Time & Life Pictures/Getty Images; p. 42 Kevork Djansezian/Getty Images; p. 51 U.S. National Park Service; p. 52 Steve Northup/ Time & Life Pictures/Getty Images; p. 60 Michael Nagle/Getty Images; pp. 62, 67 Boston Globe/Getty Images; pp. 70–71 Missouri Department of Corrections/AP Images: p. 83 Stan Honda/AFP/Getty Images; p. 87 Mark Wilson/Getty Images; page and text box border images © iStockphoto.com/Wayne Howard (crowd & flag), © iStockphoto.com/DHuss (U. S. Capitol building), © iStockphoto.com/Andrea Gingerich (faces).

Designer: Les Kanturek; Editor: Kathy Kuhtz Campbell; Photo Researcher: Amy Feinberg

Hopkinsville-Christian County Public Library

1101 BETHEL STREET

HOPKINSVILLE, KENTUCKY 42240